TAKING STOCK OF
Taking Liberties

TAKING STOCK OF
Taking Liberties

A Personal View
Linda Colley

BRITISH LIBRARY

First published 2008 by

The British Library

96 Euston Road

London NW1 2DB

Text © 2008 Linda Colley

Images © The British Library Board and other named copyright holders

British Library Cataloguing-in-Publication Data

A CIP record for this volume is available from The British Library

ISBN 978 0 7123 5041 9

Designed and typeset by Bobby Birchall

Front cover design by John Overeem

Colour reproduction by Dot Gradations Ltd., UK

Printed in England by Cromwell Press Ltd.

FRONT COVER AND TITLE PAGE: Treasure chest with Magna Carta, from *The Political House that Jack Built...*, 16th edition, London, 1819 (BL, 8135.e.1 (6)).
BACK COVER: Linda Colley © *Princeton Weekly Bulletin*.

Contents

Preface

Some years ago, I suggested to Lynne Brindley, Chief Executive of the British Library, that it should stage an exhibition about the history of political rights in these islands. She responded with typical enthusiasm and generosity, and it has been extraordinarily exciting to watch these raw, preliminary ideas evolve into *Taking Liberties*, and to serve as its guest-curator. The bulk of the work involved in preparing this exhibition, though, has been done by others. Among the many staff of the British Library who participated in some way, I wish particularly to acknowledge the contribution of Heather Norman-Soderlind, who chaired so many meetings and made time to discuss so many aspects of the show. William Frame, Arnold Hunt and Matthew Shaw devoted enormous effort, knowledge and imagination to identifying and researching an array of striking, sometimes little-known documents and objects. Alan Sterenberg played a leading part in designing and building the exhibition; and Roger Walshe, Lawrence Christensen and Jon Fawcett have devoted great effort and thought to the educational, publicity and events programmes associated with it. David Way and Belinda Wilkinson have been a delight to work with on the publication of *Taking Stock of Taking Liberties*; and I must also thank the many friends and fellow historians who helped me in its composition and argument. Particular mention should be made of Anthony Lester, QC, who made time one evening to give me a lengthy phone tutorial on the past and current state of constitutional reform in the United Kingdom.

But my best thanks must go to the British Library itself. I first visited it, in its old home, as an undergraduate in the late 1960s. Since then, like millions of other scholars and writers, I have continued to be indebted to its riches. It has been a privilege to work so closely and in a rather different capacity with an institution that calls itself British but which belongs in fact to the world.

Linda Colley, August 2008

A Personal View by Linda Colley

Taking Liberties is an exercise in recovery, reminding and revision. It brings together some of the very many documents and images that survive about arguments and struggles in these islands over rights and liberties, from Magna Carta in 1215 to the present. Here are charters, books, banners, speeches, newspapers, prints, maps, photographs, films, posters and websites drawn from England, Wales, Scotland and Ireland. Some record the actions and words of monarchs, aristocrats, politicians, major intellectuals, generals, judges and great lawyers. But many of these vivid, eloquent exhibits are to do with those possessed of little formal power or status, with men and women who resisted power in some fashion, or wanted to change how power was exercised and distributed.

Today, such documents to do with taking liberties in these islands can easily be passed over. Every year, hundreds of thousands of Americans go on pilgrimages to the rotunda of the National Archives building in Washington to view the originals of the Declaration of Independence and the US Constitution. By contrast, the people on this side of the Atlantic, it is often claimed, are too pragmatic and down to earth (and some would say too conservative) to care much for texts and statements about liberty and rights. A 'hard-headed, practical common-sense', declared a leading Labour politician in the 1940s, characterized '…the average British man and woman, who may not be good at political ideology in the Continental manner but who know very well when a shoe pinches'.[1] Such (mis)perceptions have been reinforced by the absence of a written and embedded British constitution. Notoriously, the United Kingdom (UK) differs from most modern states in possessing no single document setting out the fundamentals of its government, the limits on executive power within its boundaries, and the rights and duties of its individual citizens.

Yet men and women throughout these islands have been fiercely preoccupied at intervals both with righting perceived wrongs, and with writing down and laying claim to rights. Nothing

Author's Note
The numbers in square brackets refer to the exhibits displayed in *Taking Liberties*, listed on pp.44–48.

approaching a single British constitution on paper has existed since
the drafting of the Instrument of Government in 1653–4 and the
Humble Petition and Advice in 1657. There are, though, a multiplicity
of legal and political texts, manifestos, speeches and images to do
with rights, liberties and struggle. By putting a selection of these on
show, *Taking Liberties* is out to challenge some familiar assumptions.
By implication, it also raises some increasingly pertinent questions.

For centuries, it was widely believed that, to a unique degree,
'liberty [was] the foundation of everything' in Britain.[2] Yet, as this
exhibition shows, the struggle for rights and freedoms throughout
these islands (and not simply in Ireland) has in reality been a
protracted, fluctuating, and sometimes violent one, and
arguably is still incomplete. Why was this? How was liberty
able to become an English, and subsequently a British
shibboleth long before revolutionaries in America and
France laid claim to it, when the struggle for rights
here was so slow at times and bitter? And why,
having generated so many early, influential
constitutional statements, and exported Bills of
Rights and constitutions to many parts of its onetime
overseas empire, has the UK entered the 21st century
without a written constitution of its own, or its own
modern Bill of Rights?

There was a time when the story of taking liberties in these
islands could appear a straightforward one. Consider the
cult that grew up around Magna Carta [1]. This was wrested
from King John by his barons and catered to their sectional
interests. But since the charter also imposed limits on
supreme authority and contained evocative phrases like
'free man', it proved infinitely adaptable and politically
useful in later centuries. John Bradshaw, Lord President of

The seal of Magna Carta,
1215 (BL, Add. MS 4838).

the court that tried Charles I, invoked the 'Great Old Charter' in sentencing the king to death in 1649 [19]. In 1771, an anonymous author published a 'second Magna Charta' calling for forty-eight representatives from the American colonies (including some for the 'Indian Nations') to be allotted seats at the Westminster Parliament. The Reform Act of 1832, which reconfigured and amended the UK's representative system, was widely interpreted – by artists as well as writers – as a new 'Great Charter, in which our rights are inscribed in terms never to be erased'. And, in 1833, when Westminster passed legislation providing for the phasing out of slavery throughout the British Empire, abolitionists promptly hailed this Emancipation Act as a 'Magna Carta for negro rights'. Runnymede, the site where Magna Carta was sealed, was viewed, indeed, as such a sacred political and patriotic site that the National Trust purchased it in 1930.[3] Even in 1946, a British minister, John Balfour, could hail the charter of the new United Nations as merely the most recent of Magna Carta's 'authentic offspring'. He went on to claim for his own country a lineage of freedom 'without equal in human history'.[4] According to this way of looking at things, British political arrangements had always proved especially favourable to liberty, which had evolved here since the distant past in a triumphantly linear fashion. Yet the chronology of taking liberties in these islands (like the geography) has been complicated and uneven. Intervals of dramatic action involving protest and political change were interspersed over the centuries with periods of relative quiet, complacency, reaction and sometimes repression. And the degree of freedom individuals have been able to enjoy has often been determined by their level of wealth, and by the nature of their religious allegiance, gender and ethnic origins.

This emerges clearly from the story this exhibition tells about voting in these islands. Despite the bribery, coercion and carnival drunkenness that William Hogarth satirized so powerfully in his election series of prints in the 1750s, early modern *England's* electoral system, at least in terms of access to the franchise, was impressive by

William Hogarth, *Four Prints of an Election: Chairing the Members, Plate 4*, London, 1758. This satire on the Oxfordshire election of 1754 suggests both the violence and corruption of some 18th-century English elections, and the licence and enjoyment they could give to women and men, poor and wealthy (British Museum, S,2.135).

contemporary European standards [36]. During the 17th and early
18th centuries, a quarter, perhaps even a third of adult Englishmen
may have been able to vote for representatives at Westminster. North
of the border, the situation was very different. So powerful were
municipal oligarchies and landowner control in Scotland, that less
than one per cent of its population was enfranchised even at the end
of the 18th century. The Reform Bills passed in 1832 [46] transformed
Scotland's political landscape, expanding its electorate sixteen-fold,
and creating half a million new voters throughout Great Britain as
a whole.[5]

As a result, a higher proportion of the male population in
Britain (though not in Ireland) became enfranchised than in almost
any other European state. But the parliamentary vote remained
confined to men possessed of some property; and, after 1850, the
UK increasingly lagged behind other parts of Europe, the USA, and
even some of its own colonial dominions in the access it afforded to
the franchise. Despite new Reform Acts in 1867 and 1884, the UK
electorate at the start of the 20th century was one of the narrowest
in Europe. Almost half of Glasgow's male population, for instance,
could not vote.[6] Far from witnessing distinctive progress towards an
ever-brighter liberty, then, as far as voting rights were concerned, the
UK's record was historically mixed and in the Victorian and Edwardian
eras decidedly unimpressive by Western standards. Many of the
English, Welsh, Scottish and Irish men who volunteered to fight in
1914 at the outbreak of the First World War, can never have had any
direct experience of exercising democratic rights.

The situation of their countrywomen was in some respects
worse. To be sure, it would be wrong and anachronistic when touring
Taking Liberties to focus exclusively on the vote. For centuries, the
crucial liberties for most people were probably not franchise rights,
but rather freedom from tyranny at home, freedom from foreign
invasion, freedom of conscience and worship, and security of
property. If she was Protestant, a spinster or widow, or possessed a

'The Ladies' Advocate',
cartoon from *Punch*, 1 June,
1867 (BL, PP.5270.ah).

good marriage settlement, and was at least modestly prosperous, a
woman in 17th-, 18th-, and 19th-century England, Wales, Scotland
and Ireland might well feel as secure in these essential liberties as her
male neighbours. And those few women who owned a landed estate
or a substantial business in their own right could exercise more
electoral clout than most men. True, they had no parliamentary vote
of their own. But, before the advent of the secret ballot in 1872,
wealthy women of this sort – like wealthy men – were often able at
election time to sway the votes of male employees and dependants.

Nonetheless, the degree to which many of the exhibits in *Taking
Liberties* are bluntly or tacitly gendered is striking. Some of the soldiers
and officers from Oliver Cromwell's New Model Army who took part
in the Putney Debates of 1647 argued impressively in support of even
the 'poorest he that is in England' having the right to consent to the
government under which he lived [27]. None of them, however, seem
to have made explicit reference to the rights of 'she'.[7] 'John Bull', a
caricatured male plebeian, often features in 18th-century English prints
claiming liberty or attacking oppression; but he had no graphic female
counterpart. And although there were many female supporters of
Chartism at the movement's outset, none of the three massive Chartist
petitions for universal male suffrage submitted to Parliament in the
1830s and 1840s mentioned votes for women [56–57]. In May 1867,
the Liberal MP and philosopher John Stuart Mill tried to persuade the
House of Commons to replace references to 'man' in the Reform Bill
of that year with 'person', so as to smuggle propertied women
into the franchise. This failed, as would every other pre-1914
parliamentary initiative in support of women's suffrage.[8]

Hence the foundation in 1897 of the National Union of
Women's Suffrage Societies to coordinate extra-parliamentary
pressure across the United Kingdom – and the tactics employed by a
breakaway group, the Women's Social and Political Union (WSPU).
Dubbed 'Suffragettes' by hostile journalists, some of these more
militant women poured acid into letter boxes, committed arson,

PUNCH, OR THE LONDON CHARIVARI.—June 1, 1867.

THE LADIES' ADVOCATE.

Mrs. Bull. "LOR, MR. MILL! WHAT A LOVELY SPEECH YOU *DID* MAKE. I DO DECLARE I HADN'T THE SLIGHTEST NOTION WE WERE SUCH MISERABLE CREATURES. NO ONE CAN SAY IT WAS *YOUR* FAULT THAT THE CASE BROKE DOWN."

The Daily Herald

No. 346. [REGISTERED AT THE G.P.O. AS A NEWSPAPER.] SATURDAY, MAY 24, 1913. ONE HALFPENNY.

" For what you are about to receive . . . ."

[Mr. McKenna, Forcible-Feeder-in-Chief to the Cabinet, has described with moving candour the loving and chivalrous care, the almost pious delicacy, with which the Government treats those of its Suffragist enemies who fall into its tender hands.]

McKENNA, F.-F.-In-C. (to the World at Large):—
" Observe how we treat every case
With the Chivalrous Tact of our Race—
How before we proceed
To forcibly feed,
We NEVER omit to say Grace!"

A profoundly ambivalent
spoof on the force-feeding
of imprisoned 'Suffragettes'
from the *Daily Herald,* 24 May
1913 (BL, 1911–14 LON
MLD5 NPL).

smashed windows, and physically assaulted cabinet ministers in a fashion that might now get them labelled terrorists [65–78]. The authorities reacted by force-feeding Suffragette prisoners who went on hunger strike, and secretly spied on and photographed them in their cells.[9] Whether the Suffragettes' campaigns aided or damaged the cause of female enfranchisement remains in dispute. The violence surrounding these women is unquestionably significant for what it reveals about the markedly strong passions that early female emancipation aroused in the UK. Olive Wharry, a Suffragette whose scrapbook of drawings and poems forms part of this exhibition, weighed less than 35.8 kg (79 lbs) when she was let out of Holloway jail; she also planted bombs in Kew Gardens [72]. Not until 1928, did women in the UK secure the vote on the same terms as men; and not until the 1990s, did the number of female MPs at Westminster begin to approach the proportion of female legislators already achieved in many other European and non-European states.[10]

The often snail-like advance of male and, even more, female enfranchisement is a warning against any simple and self-congratulatory interpretation of the taking of liberties in these islands. Claims of precocious British legal and political freedoms can also be criticized for being – in two senses at least – unduly Anglocentric.

First, because in stressing that this was 'a land, perhaps the only one in the universe, in which political or civil liberty is the very end and scope of the constitution', such patriotic legends glossed over how much reformers in England, Wales, Scotland and Ireland have always derived ideas and inspiration from other parts of the world.[11] Thus there are powerful domestic reasons for the inclusion in this exhibition of Thomas Paine's *Rights of Man* (1791–2). Over a million people in Britain and Ireland may have read this two-part work in the 1790s, and it was a vital inspiration for the brief flourishing of Corresponding Societies, groups of artisans, workers and professionals committed to securing universal male suffrage [112–13].[12] But the *Rights of Man* was also an international text. In retrospect, indeed, it

A copy of the Declaration of Arbroath, composed in 1320, possibly by Bernard de Linton, Chancellor of Scotland: 'Never will we on any conditions be brought under English rule' (National Archives of Scotland, SP13/7).

is a global text, since it pioneered the phrase 'human rights'. Many of Paine's ideas and even his writing style were derived from his time in Revolutionary America and the new Republic, and he was also influenced by his subsequent visits to France. His advocacy of old age pensions in Part II of the *Rights*, for instance, shows the influence of the French philosopher and economist, the Marquis de Condorcet. There were many other transnational and transcontinental reformist and radical borrowings. Those late 19th- and early 20th-century Irish nationalists who argued for a new Irish Bill of Rights took some of their ideas from contemporary Indian nationalists in the Congress party who wanted a Bill of Rights for an independent India.[13]

This points to the second respect in which traditional paeans to British liberty could be Anglocentric: they often paid insufficient attention to Welsh, Scottish and Irish differences, and only selective attention to Britain's overseas empire, a topic I will touch on later. Although many of its exhibits are of English provenance, *Taking Liberties* offers examples of how the pursuit of rights was sometimes experienced very differently in the so-called Celtic Fringe countries, and could find expression in struggles to be free of England or to diminish London's control and interference [e.g. 82, 85, 103, 104].

Such disparities and divisions were hardly surprising, since Great Britain and, still more, the United Kingdom are comparatively recent constructs. Although successive Anglo-Norman monarchs strove to leave an imprint on Wales and Scotland and, after 1170, on Ireland, parliamentary union between England and Wales – very much on London's terms – only took place in the 1530s and 1540s. By contrast, it was a Scot who was responsible for first linking England, Wales and Scotland in a dynastic union. In 1603, King James VI of Scotland also inherited the thrones of England and Ireland [89–90]. The making of England, Wales and Scotland into 'one united kingdom by the name of Great Britain', with (until recently) a single legislature at Westminster, was only achieved through the Treaty of Union of 1707 [93–4]. The Act of Union of 1800 effected a further change of name and

political organization by establishing the United Kingdom of Great Britain and Ireland, abolishing the Irish Parliament at Dublin, and admitting 100 Irish MPs to Westminster. After the Irish Revolution, and the creation of the Irish Free State in 1922 (subsequently the Republic of Ireland), the title of this conglomerate became instead the United Kingdom of Great Britain and Northern Ireland.[14]

Varieties of Welsh, Scottish and Irish could possess rather different reasons in the past for *sometimes* viewing issues to do with rights and liberties differently from the English, and differently too from each other. Even in the late 19th century, three out of four people in Wales remained monolingual Welsh speakers or spoke Welsh out of choice, so for a long time direct access to English-language political texts in this part of the island was limited. North of the border, the nature of political debate was always influenced by the fact that Scots retained their own legal system after the Treaty of Union, their own church organization and ancient universities, and before 1707 (as again now) their own Parliament at Edinburgh. But it was in Ireland, where political differences and deprivations were often – though not always – most stark. Separated from Britain by the sea and, after the Protestant Reformation, by its majority religion, Ireland was also subjected to successive invasions by land-hungry Norman, English and Scottish adventurers. Its Parliament at Dublin was increasingly run by the Protestant landed and professional elite, and generally kept subordinate to the Westminster Parliament. By the time of the Union in 1800, many Protestant Irish and some middle-class and landed Irish Catholics were prepared, out of conviction or self-interest, to share in the celebration of 'British' liberties. This could not be the case, however, with the mass of the Irish rural poor. Their overwhelming Catholicism, and the poverty to which this often contributed, proved grievous disabilities in a polity that had cause to boast of its religious freedom, but – from the late 1500s until 1829 – chiefly in regard to those of its people who were Protestants [181, 182, 186].

Yet struggles to take liberties have repeatedly crossed borders,

and have fostered unities as well as underlining differences. Scottish
Whigs in the late 17th, 18th and 19th centuries, for instance, were
quite as enthusiastic as their English counterparts about celebrating the
destruction of Charles I and his 'tyranny', because their countrymen
had made a signal contribution to overthrowing the monarch. In 1638,
large numbers of nobles, gentry, burgesses and clergymen in Edinburgh
and elsewhere in Scotland had signed copies of a National Covenant in
protest at attempts by Charles I and his ministers to interfere in the
Scottish Kirk [91]. This campaign helped to precipitate the civil wars of the
1640s and to secure the victory of Parliament's armies. As one Scottish
historian boasted: 'Every Scottishman ought to look [at the National
Covenant] with as great reverence as Englishmen do to the Magna
Charta. It is what saved the country from despotism'.[15] Later struggles
for wider rights too were often British-wide, and sometimes UK-wide.

   Thus the Corresponding Society movement of the 1790s started
in London and the English provinces, but soon spilled over into Wales
and Scotland. In the 1830s and 1840s, radical newspapers and
lecturers and the new railways spread the Chartist message across
the kingdom. There were lethal Chartist riots in parts of Wales, major
Chartist demonstrations in Scotland, and some of the movement's
most conspicuous leaders were Irish professionals and MPs. Hence
the inclusion in the second Chartist petition to Westminster in 1842
of a demand that the Act of Union between Britain and Ireland be
repealed.[16] As this suggests, dissidents and campaigners across these
islands have regularly worked in tandem and pooled ideas and tactics,
while also sometimes pursuing more distinct objectives depending on
their country of origin. Thus the General Strike of 1926, called to
secure coal miners a living wage, was organized by the British Trades
Union Congress (TUC) and focused on London [159]. But the strike
also found especially angry expression in Glasgow, where there was
a local tradition of militant trade unionism, and in Cardiff, where the
proximity of the South Wales collieries made the plight of coal miners
a particularly emotive and patriotic issue.[17]

The political and human realities, then, were often less impressive and infinitely more complex than the ringing rhetoric and celebration that once surrounded the idea of British liberty. To this extent, the sheer abundance of impassioned print and writings in this exhibition can be read less as a testimony to the long rooted-ness of freedom in these islands, than as evidence of how hard and long for some has been the struggle to take and secure liberties.

Yet, for all this, the rhetoric and ideology of liberty do matter. They matter because some of the texts on show in *Taking Liberties* were profoundly innovative, and have worked to aid and expand human freedoms. Magna Carta, for instance, seems to have been a more ambitious attempt to impose curbs on royal authority than analogous documents produced in other early medieval European kingdoms.[18] By the same token, the Habeas Corpus Acts of 1640 and 1679 remain some of the greatest achievements of 17th-century English lawyers and parliamentarians [8–15]. Other rights are of little use if an individual can be arbitrarily kept in detention. To be sure, and as recent events have underlined, George Bernard Shaw's acid comment that British governments 'always suspended' habeas corpus whenever 'it threatened to be of the slightest use' is not without some force.[19] Yet there has been persistent value in having a formal, written commitment to the principle of habeas corpus against which the conduct of British politicians and judges could be measured. And because the UK was once an imperial power that exported its legal conventions, habeas corpus exists in the constitutions of many other countries, including India, Australia, New Zealand, the USA, Canada, Trinidad, the Bahamas and more.

The rhetoric of liberty also matters because it has been far more than 'ruling-class chatter': the stuff only of legal pronouncements, parliamentary speeches, and learned tomes. Throughout these islands, rights-talk has also been an evolving part of the politics of the street, the pubs, the chapels and churches, the clubs and print. This is underlined by the sheer diversity of printed material *Taking Liberties*

Politically subversive tobacco paper printed in 1792, three years after the outbreak of the French Revolution (BL, Add. MS 16922).

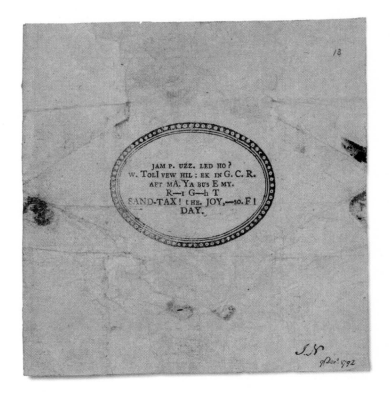

is able to display: not only books, pamphlets and newspapers, but also cartoons, advertisements, posters, handbills, ballads, maps, electoral addresses, proclamations, even seditious tobacco papers [119]. The volume and range of printed material produced in these islands grew exponentially after the lapsing of the Licensing Act in 1695; and, along with improvements in transport and the postal system, this fostered a much wider dissemination of political information and ideas. Crucially, cheap, widely produced and widely-distributed print made it easier for political activists in one part of Britain or the UK to learn about, and co-ordinate action with fellow sympathizers in other regions. Thus, in 1840, radically minded readers in the English city of Leeds could purchase a local edition of the life of the Chartist martyr John Frost 'tried by special commission at Monmouth in Wales' [59].

Interesting Life, and Important
Eight Day's Trial of John Frost,
for High Treason... Leeds, 1840
(BL, 1578/805(1)).

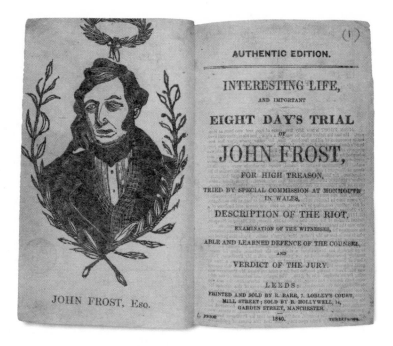

But, long before 1695 and the proliferation of print, rights-talk had expanded beyond the uses only of the powerful and the formally educated. An historically suspect but fertile idea developed early that Magna Carta had restored only *some* of the freedoms once enjoyed by Anglo-Saxons and Ancient Britons. These original freedoms, it was argued, had been suppressed when the Normans invaded England in 1066. Consequently, striving to restore these 'lost' freedoms was a legitimate and needful work in progress. This was what the Levellers meant in the mid-1600s when they spoke of wanting 'to recover our birthright'. Far from expressing complacency, claiming that British liberties were peculiarly ancient and innate could thus be a means of advancing and sanctioning demands for change.[20] When Joseph Gerrald was hauled before the Edinburgh courts in 1793 and accused of sedition for supporting universal manhood suffrage and popular resistance, he took his stand not on the radicalism of his demands, but on customary and inviolable rights. 'In the established usages of our ancestors, we sought for precedent, and we found it', he told the

A poster issued by the
National Union of Women's
Suffrage Societies in 1913
(BL, 8413.k.5).

members of the jury: 'You are Britons – you are freemen'.[21] Essentially
the same tactic of citing supposed ancient national rights in order
to push novel claims in fact is evident in a 1913 Suffragist poster:
'Be Wise, Be Fair, Be Just, *Be British*, and ask your Members of
Parliament to vote for Women's Suffrage'.

Appealing to the powerful in such terms could sometimes work. As the historian Edmund Morgan has written, all governments and rulers rely on certain vaunted fictions: be it the divine right of kings, or the sovereignty of the people, or a people's republic, or an ancient, unwritten, but peculiarly free British constitution. And while such fictions 'enable the few to govern the many', it is not only the many who are affected. If the fiction is to work and compel mass belief, rulers and governments may also be obliged at times to sacrifice a measure of the freedom and power they would otherwise enjoy.[22] One of the best examples of liberty being invoked to sway and constrain elite action in this fashion was the campaign to persuade Westminster to ban British involvement in the transatlantic slave trade.

For as long as black slaves could be viewed as merchandise, as chattels rather than as human beings, the denial of their most basic rights was generally not viewed as being at odds with British pretensions to superior liberty. In the 1600s and the first half of the 18th century, the Westminster Parliament and the English and Scottish courts repeatedly found in favour of slave ownership and slave trading. But after the Somerset case in 1772, when Granville Sharp appealed successfully for a writ of habeas corpus to prevent a black slave from being recovered by his onetime owner and shipped out of the country, prevailing language and opinion increasingly shifted. The presiding judge in the Somerset case, Lord Mansfield, seems to have viewed his verdict as a cautious and strictly legalistic one.[23] But this was not how it was universally interpreted. Instead, sections of the newspaper press, anti-slavery activists, and the slave at the centre of the affair – James Somerset – claimed that Mansfield's decision meant that slaves brought into Britain would have to be freed. 'In Britain', trumpeted the Welsh radical Dr. Richard Price, 'a negro becomes a freeman the moment he sets his foot on British ground'. Contact with British soil and consequently with British liberties, so the argument went, was *ipso facto* bound to liberate. By the end of the 18th century, some abolitionists were also routinely describing slaves transported in British slave-ships as 'fellow subjects' or 'British subjects', and consequently as beings who again necessarily possessed a claim on British legal protections and freedoms.[24]

Such assertions continued to be contested in the courts, but re-describing slaves in this fashion proved an adroit abolitionist strategy. It played on how large numbers of ordinary Britons – and many among the British ruling elite – wanted to see themselves and their state: as conspicuously benevolent, peculiarly free, a beacon and example to the world. There were many reasons why Westminster voted to pull out of the still very profitable transatlantic slave trade in 1806–7, and why British governments subsequently invested a great deal of revenue and naval effort in suppressing slaving in other parts of the world. One of them was the conviction among many UK officials that, in the light of British liberty, this was the only plausible policy. The prevailing fictions seemed now to provide for no other way of acting.

As the campaign over the slave trade suggests, an exhibition devoted to taking liberties in these islands would ideally range across the globe. British and Irish radicals and reformers have repeatedly borrowed ideas and tactics from other countries and continents. And, from the 1500s at least, arguments and initiatives about rights at home were often intertwined with debates and controversies about power and liberties in the empire. There is only space to touch on some of the ways in which this was so.

At one level, 'the articulation of a humane regime of law and rights' could serve as a means of legitimating British invasions and occupations overseas, and as a way of distinguishing British actions from those of rival empires. Claims that the Ottoman, Spanish, Chinese, or Russian empires were oppressive, whereas the British were engaged in exporting the rule of law and wider human rights to less fortunate lands, were a persistent part both of Britain's ideology of liberty and of its ideology of empire.[25] The empire also

Two views of British Empire: The empire as constitutional tutor
('The Dominion Tie', *Punch*, 11 June 1947), and the empire as
a reluctant conceder of rights ('Spoiling the Daughter-in-law',
Hindi Punch, January 1892 (BL, PP.5270.ah and BL, 1876.b.61).

Punch, June 11 1947

THE DOMINION TIE

"Good-bye and good luck—and don't forget there's quite a flourishing Old Boys' Society you might
care to join."

INDIAN NATIONAL CONGRESS CARTOONS FROM THE "HINDI PUNCH."

SPOILING THE DAUGHTER-IN-LAW.

(SEVENTH INDIAN NATIONAL CONGRESS,—NAGPUR, 28th DECEMBER, 1891.)

Lady Congress.—Mother-in-law dear, will you never train me up in my household duties? It is neither dignified nor prudent that you should grind all the day long, and I simply look on.

[*Hindi Punch, Jan., 1892.*]

impacted over the centuries on much domestic rights legislation. The Habeas Corpus Act of 1679, for instance, was partly designed to prevent English and Welsh civilians from being arbitrarily sent into indentured servitude in colonies and settlements in North America and North Africa.[26]

Britain's empire could also serve as a warning. Its officials and troops frequently outraged freedoms overseas in a manner that would have been unthinkable in the island of Britain itself.[27] Martial law was never attempted in Britain after 1780 (though it was in Ireland), but it was resorted to in British Canada in 1837–8, in British Jamaica in 1831 and 1865, in South Africa in 1899–1901, and in many other colonial contexts. One of the persistent criticisms levelled against the empire by reformers and jurists was that such abuses overseas might in due course threaten and infect the quality of liberties at home. It was vital, argued Lord Chief Justice Alexander Cockburn in London in 1867, that 'every British citizen, white, brown, or black in skin' should be 'subject to definite, and not indefinite power'. Because otherwise, he went on (and his ordering of locations is suggestive), what was 'done in a colony today may be done in Ireland tomorrow, and in England hereafter'.[28]

Yet it bears repeating that a fervent civil religion of liberty has worked at different times to constrain and shape the actions of British governing elites, and this could also be the case in regard to the overseas empire. Thus, in 1950, the UK government signed the European Convention on Human Rights. Moreover, in 1953, the British extended this Convention to their remaining colonial dependencies, with results that sometimes proved inconvenient to their own subsequent authority in these colonies. Once again, the rhetoric and ideology of liberty were shown to matter.[29]

How much do they matter in these islands now? The philosopher Isaiah Berlin famously distinguished between two concepts of liberty:

negative liberty meaning an absence of obstacles and restraints, and liberty as the freedom to choose and advance positive goals.[30] In the 20th and early 21st centuries, the inhabitants of the UK have witnessed extensive gains in both modes of liberty.

In 1900, a substantial minority of men over twenty-one and all women in England, Wales, Scotland and Ireland were still excluded from the parliamentary franchise. Now, virtually every male and female citizen of the UK over eighteen has the vote, though many fail to use it. In 1900, average life expectancy at birth in the UK was about forty. Now, in part because of the introduction of old age pensions and the National Health Service, average life expectancy for both sexes in these islands has almost doubled [176–7]. And equality and respect for human differences are now guiding principles in parliamentary legislation and in the ordering of the state to a degree that would have been unthinkable in 1900 – or at any earlier period. At one level, this means that individuals who are gay, female, physically challenged, non-white, elderly, or not Christian are less likely (though not yet entirely *un*likely) to experience discrimination or persecution without some form of redress [eg. 137–40]. At a wider level, Catholics in Northern Ireland now enjoy a much fairer share of its resources, jobs, and educational and political opportunities; and all of the inhabitants of this part of the UK, together with the Welsh and Scots have secured greater rights of self-government. In 1998, the Good Friday Agreement and devolution legislation provided for the re-establishment of a Northern Ireland Assembly at Belfast, and for the foundation of a Welsh Assembly at Cardiff and a new Scottish Parliament at Edinburgh [106].[31]

But the converse of these developments is also important. The rise in welfare provision since 1900 and of legislation on behalf of various minorities and the vulnerable bears witness to, and has helped to accelerate an unprecedented expansion in the reach of the state. Until the later 1800s, the civilian wing of the British state was compact by European standards, because health, education, housing,

THE
MILITARY SERVICE ACT,
1916,

APPLIES TO UNMARRIED MEN WHO, ON AUGUST 15th, 1915, WERE 18 YEARS OF AGE OR OVER AND WHO WILL NOT BE 41 YEARS OF AGE ON MARCH 2nd, 1916.

ALL MEN (NOT EXCEPTED OR EXEMPTED),

between the above ages who, on November 2nd, 1915, were Unmarried or Widowers without any Child dependent on them will, on

Thursday, March 2nd, 1916

BE DEEMED TO BE ENLISTED FOR THE PERIOD OF THE WAR.

They will be placed in the Reserve until Called Up in their Class.

MEN EXCEPTED:

SOLDIERS, including Territorials who have volunteered for Foreign Service;
MEN serving in the NAVY or ROYAL MARINES;
MEN DISCHARGED from ARMY or NAVY, disabled or ill, or TIME-EXPIRED MEN;
MEN REJECTED for the ARMY since AUGUST 14th, 1915;
CLERGYMEN, PRIESTS, and MINISTERS OF RELIGION;
VISITORS from the DOMINIONS.

MEN WHO MAY BE EXEMPTED BY LOCAL TRIBUNALS:

Men more useful to the Nation in their present employments;
Men in whose case Military Service would cause serious hardship owing to exceptional financial or business obligations or domestic position;
Men who are ill or infirm;
Men who conscientiously object to combatant service. If the Tribunal thinks fit, men may, on this ground, be (*a*) exempted from combatant service only (not non-combatant service), or (*b*) exempted on condition that they are engaged in work of National importance.

Up to March 2nd, a man can apply to his Local Tribunal for a certificate of exemption. There is a Right of Appeal. He will not be called up until his case has been dealt with finally.

Certificates of exemption may be absolute, conditional or temporary. Such certificates can be renewed, varied or withdrawn.

Men retain their Civil Rights until called up and are amenable to Civil Courts only.

DO NOT WAIT UNTIL MARCH 2nd.
ENLIST VOLUNTARILY NOW.

For fuller particulars of the Act, please apply for Leaflet No. 64 to the nearest Post Office, Police Station, or Recruiting Office.

Published by THE PARLIAMENTARY RECRUITING COMMITTEE, LONDON.—Poster No. 155. Wt. 1406/246.   Printed by ROBERTS & LEETE, Ld., London.

Rising state power
encroaching on rights: The
Military Service Act of 1916
provided for conscription in
the UK for the first time
(Imperial War Museum,
PST 5161).

the environment, care of the old etc. were rarely central government concerns. Even in 1910, there were just twenty-seven clerks at work collecting data in the newly created Pensions Office in London. By 1946, however, the provincial records branch alone of the Ministry of Pensions employed almost 4000 staff.[32] Since the Second World War, governments have also increasingly been able to use technology in order to monitor and micro-manage. Some of these new technologies, like CCTV cameras on roads, are controversial. But other high-tech intrusions by agents of the state into what, in earlier ages, would have been considered individuals' private business, have become taken for granted, an accepted part of the background of life. Taxes, for instance, are now commonly deducted at source even before people receive their wages. As one scholar remarks, had a 'revenue system of such scope and power' been available in the 13th century, 'it is most unlikely that King John would have…been forced to sign Magna Carta'.[33]

The massively increased power that modern governments possess to monitor and regulate their citizens, and the potential challenges this poses to individual liberties and privacy, are scarcely conditions that are unique to the UK. However, the exponential rise in state power does arguably underline some persistent deficiencies in the UK's political system.

As *Taking Liberties* illustrates, the British were precociously successful by European standards in curbing the power of their monarchs. They have been less successful – and less concerned – in curbing the executive in terms of the powers enjoyed by ministers, and the power that governments can normally exert over the conduct and decision-making of the House of Commons. The idea has long flourished, and been nourished by the cult of British liberty, that 'because Parliament was the protector of the people's rights, it could be no threat to them'.[34] Yet, as a succession of political commentators has pointed out since the late 17th century, the possibility always exists of the Westminster Parliament becoming 'a mere state engine

Rising state power and
improved provision of welfare:
The Social Insurance plan of
1944 (BL, 1899.ss.18 (74)).

in the hands of a minister, to stamp a value on the basest metal, and
to give every bad measure the sanction of national consent'. The
House of Commons usually (though not always) does the bidding
of the Prime Minister of the day. Especially if the ruling party has a
comfortable majority, the Commons 'can force through Parliament
and obtain the Crown's assent to legislation which the executive
wants: neither the Crown nor the Lords, and certainly not the judges,
can stop the executive getting the legislation it wants'.[35] As effective
head of the executive, a prime minister can be politically overturned
by opposition parties in the Commons, or by members of his or her
own party; but no binding and comprehensive statement exists as to
how prime ministers of the United Kingdom may or may not use their
power. Nor, so long as their political party continues to win general
elections, are there any legal limits at present on how long British
prime ministers may hold office.

How does one account for these constitutional silences and
omissions, given the many innovatory texts and initiatives to do with
power and rights that were generated in these islands in earlier
periods? In part, the answer is that the good can be an enemy of the
best. Parliament's success in binding successive monarchs, plus its
members' vaunted concern for securing liberties, provided for a long
time for widespread, though never unanimous, patriotic complacency
about the existing political and parliamentary system. So did events
overseas and ideologies at home. During the late 18th and 19th
centuries, the countries that were most notable for having
comprehensive and innovatory written constitutions were post-
Revolutionary France and the USA [110–11]. Both of these powers
were republics, and both fought massive wars against Britain in the
process of becoming so. Consequently, it was easy and tempting for
many members of the British governing class – and for many ordinary
Britons – to view written constitutions too as suspect artefacts and as
quintessentially alien [eg. 117].

The Tree of LIBERTY,—with, the Devil tempting John Bull.

Political innovation
represented as foreign and
sterile: James Gillray's *The Tree
of LIBERTY, – with the Devil
tempting John Bull'*, London,
1798 (British Museum,
1868.0808/6739).

The idea that paper guarantees of fundamental rights and
written constitutions were probably worthless and possibly dangerous
was further encouraged by the writings of three major political and
legal theorists: Edmund Burke (1729–97), Jeremy Bentham
(1748–1832) and Albert Venn Dicey (1835–1922). Burke, in his
parliamentary speeches and in *Reflections on the Revolution in
France* (1790) famously denounced the revolution for having 'tore to
pieces the contexture of the state', and poured scorn on reformers
who embraced doctrines of natural rights and plotted political change
in accordance with 'abstract rules' [116]. Bentham's politics were more
radical. But he, too, reacted against the French Revolution and
dismissed natural rights theory as 'simple nonsense'. An advocate of
universal male and female suffrage (subject only to a literacy test), his
ideal was an omni-competent legislature that might implement useful
reforms of benefit to the greatest possible number of people. This,
rather than statements of individual liberties, was the desirable goal in
government. Dicey, who was Professor of English law at Oxford
University, was a far less original and powerful thinker. Like Burke and
Bentham, however, he influenced generations of British politicians,
jurists and civil servants, in part because his arguments were at once
impressively lucid and congenial to conventional patriots. Dicey's
Introduction to the Study of the Law of the Constitution (1885),
which went through many editions, stressed the importance of the
rule of law and of parliamentary sovereignty, and the need to respect
Britain's existing and historic constitutional conventions.[36]

The prolonged influence of these and allied writings can be
traced in the responses of both British domestic and colonial
politicians and officials. Thus, in 1935, British constitutional lawyers
rejected a demand for a Bill of Rights to be included in the
Government of India Act of that year on the grounds that it 'would
either be a string of empty platitudes or a handicap to effective
legislation'. The scepticism about natural rights and paper guarantees
that was part of the legacy of Burke, Bentham and Dicey can,

Human Rights Act, 1998
(Parliamentary Archives).

perhaps, even be detected in some recent media and parliamentary responses to the Human Rights Act (HRA) of 1998. This enshrined rights that had previously been protected by the European Convention on Human Rights, including the right to life, prohibition of torture, freedom of expression, the right to education, and the right to free elections [136]. But even though such aims are scarcely controversial, and even though British lawyers played an important role in drafting the original European Convention on Human Rights, the HRA has been attacked by some journalists and politicians in almost Burkeian terms: as intrinsically foreign, as nonsensical and pernicious, as 'nothing more than something that "criminals and grasping lawyers bend to their own advantage"'.[37]

Yet, for many men and women in the past, the most powerful and visceral arguments for constitutional conservatism were probably the UK's relative stability and prosperity, and its formidable capacity to win wars and to resist invasion. In the 1860s, for example, the UK was at the height of its economic and imperial primacy. By contrast, France and the USA, the two great exponents of radical written constitution-making, spent much of that decade convulsed by invasion, revolution, or civil war. At the end of the Second World War, in 1945, most Continental European states lay in ruins and the UK itself was greatly reduced. Nonetheless, the latter remained apparently amongst the winners, its political ordering and parliamentary system still intact and vindicated once more.

But if nothing succeeds like success, it is no less true that few things are more unsettling than perceived failures and frailties. As relief and pride at the UK's victory in the war has gradually receded, as realization has sunk in of its relative economic decline and reduced global clout, and as its society has become more pluralistic, so debate about political and constitutional changes and individual rights of different kinds has become steadily more vociferous. Discussion of such topics has by now moved far beyond pressure groups such as Charter 88. At the time of writing (August 2008), the House of Lords

Human Rights Act 1998

AN ACT

TO

Give further effect to rights and freedoms guaranteed under the European Convention on Human Rights; to make provision with respect to holders of certain judicial offices who become judges of the European Court of Human Rights; and for connected purposes.

Chapter 42   **9th November 1998**

is set to debate the constitutional and legal appropriateness of detaining terrorist suspects for forty-two days without charge, while simultaneously being itself subject to ongoing demands for institutional reform. A Joint Committee of both Houses has recently called for the adoption of a new UK Bill of Rights that will go further than existing human rights legislation. Simultaneously, the Scottish National Party is urging its own Scottish Bill of Rights, while the Bill of Rights for Northern Ireland that was promised in the Good Friday Agreement is now under serious discussion. In Wales, the new Assembly is demanding similar legislative powers as the Edinburgh Parliament; while some English nationalists are calling for a parliament of their own, or at least for a reduction at Westminster in the influence of MPs representing constituencies outside England. Having earlier issued a white paper on 'The Governance of Britain', which announced the abandonment of some minor executive powers, the current administration is considering a Constitutional Renewal Bill, and is about to inaugurate a Supreme Court.

Such a rich mix of competing, piecemeal initiatives runs some risk of making Lord Scarman's verdict on the British constitution even more applicable in the future than when he first voiced it in 1992. The British constitution was not in fact 'unwritten', Scarman observed (and *Taking Liberties* shows the truth of this). But, he went on, the UK's constitutional conventions and its various peoples' myriad and hard-won rights were hidden away in a bewildering array of political and legal texts, and consequently 'difficult to find' and understand.[38] Whether the pace of current protests, reform proposals and would-be separatisms will culminate in some future attempt at a new constitutional synthesis for the UK cannot be known. *Taking Liberties* reveals some of the profound obstacles in the way of such an eventuality. This exhibition also suggests that a major constitutional re-configuring is not beyond the bounds of possibility.

———————————

TAKING LIBERTIES

References

1   Herbert Morrison, quoted in Ulrike Jordan and Wolfram Kaiser (eds.), *Political Reform in Britain, 1886–1996* (Bochum, 1997), p.56.

2   The view of Britain of the onetime American Revolutionary, Patrick Henry, in a speech made in June 1788 to the Virginia Convention called to ratify the Constitution of the United States.

3   Peter Linebaugh, *The Magna Carta Manifesto: Liberties and Commons for All* (Berkeley, CA, 2008), pp.70, 140, 202; *Heads of the proposed Bill, or second Magna Charta of England, mentioned in a Letter address'd to the People of Great Britain…* (1771). For sculptural and journalistic references to Magna Carta in connection with the 1832 Reform Act, see my *Britons: Forging the Nation 1707–1837* (London, 1992), pp.343–6.

4   Lord Irvine of Lairg, *Human Rights, Constitutional Law and the Development of the English Legal System: Selected Essays* (Oxford, 2003), pp.262–3.

5   T.M. Devine, *The Scottish Nation: 1700–2000* (London, 1999), pp.196, 273; for the early modern English electorate, see Derek Hirst, *The Representative of the People? Voters and Voting in England under the Stuarts* (Cambridge, 1975), and Geoffrey Holmes, *The Electorate and the National Will in the First Age of Party* (Lancaster, 1976).

6   Devine, *Scottish Nation*, p.540; and for European comparisons, see Robert J. Goldstein, *Political Repression in 19th Century Europe* (London, 1983).

7   Michael Mendle (ed.), *The Putney Debates of 1647: the Army, the Levellers, and the English State* (Cambridge, 2001) *passim;* for the possibility that some mid-17th-century radicals did think in terms of political liberties for females, see Quentin Skinner, 'Re-thinking political liberty', *History Workshop Journal* 61 (2006), especially pp.158–60.

8   Though single and widowed female ratepayers in England and Wales were able to vote for local bodies after 1869. Municipal enfranchisement was granted to women in Scotland and Ireland on similar terms in 1882 and 1898 respectively. In 1881, the Isle of Man amended its franchise to allow propertied women to vote in elections for its parliament, the House of Keys.

9 . For some of these covert photographs, see Jill Liddington, 'Era of commemoration: celebrating the suffrage centenary', *History Workshop Journal* 59 (2005), p.208.

10 See Martin Pugh, *Women and the Women's Movement in Britain 1914–1959* (Basingstoke,

1992); and Brian Harrison, 'Women in a men's house: the women M.P.s, 1919–1945', *Historical Journal* 29 (1986). At the time Harrison was writing – barely twenty years ago – the highest total of women MPs ever to sit in the House of Commons was just twenty-nine.

11 The quotation is from the great 18th-century English jurist William Blackstone: A.W. Brian Simpson, *Human Rights and the End of Empire: Britain and the Genesis of the European Convention* (Oxford, 2001), p.26.

12 The best account of Paine's domestic impact is still E.P. Thompson, *The Making of the English Working Class* (London, 1963).

13 I owe this information on the Irish nationalists and their ideas about a Bill of Rights to Lord Lester of Herne Hill, QC. For another example of transnational radical influences, see Laura E. Nym Mayhall, 'The rhetorics of slavery and citizenship: suffragist discourse and canonical texts in Britain, 1880–1914', *Gender & History* 13 (2001), which discusses the impact of the Italian nationalist, Giuseppe Mazzini, on the women's suffrage movement in the UK.

14 This and the next paragraph range across some crowded and contentious historiography. For some guidelines, see the forthcoming new edition of *Britons: Forging the Nation*; R.F. Foster, *Modern Ireland, 1600–1972* (London, 1988); Geraint H. Jenkins, *A Concise History of Wales* (Cambridge, 2007); Devine, *Scottish Nation*; and R.R. Davies, *Domination and Conquest: The Experience of Ireland, Scotland and Wales 1100–1300* (Cambridge, 1990).

15 Neil Forsyth, 'Presbyterian historians and the Scottish invention of British liberty', *Scottish Church History* 34 (2004), p.101 and *passim*.

16 See the essays in Owen Ashton *et al* (eds.), *The Chartist Legacy* (Woodbridge, 1999); and Philip Howell, '"Diffusing the light of liberty": The geography of political lecturing in the Chartist movement', *Journal of Historical Geography* 21 (1995), pp.23–38.

17 For a recent British-wide survey, see Anne Perkins, *A Very British Strike* (London, 2006).

18 See J.C. Holt, *Magna Carta* (2nd edn., Cambridge, 1992).

19 See David Clark and Gerard McCoy, *The Most Fundamental Legal Right: Habeas Corpus in the Commonwealth* (Oxford, 2000), p.1 and *passim*. It took Article 5 of the European Convention to give

new strength to the right of liberty contained in habeas corpus (*ex informatio* Lord Lester).

20 For the operation and richness of these ideas at different social and political levels, see Christopher Hill, *Puritanism and Revolution* (London, 1958); J.G.A. Pocock, *The Ancient Constitution and the Feudal Law* (Cambridge, 1957); and James H. Hutson, 'The emergence of the modern concept of a right in America', in B.A. Shain (ed.), *The Nature of Rights at the American Founding and Beyond* (London, 2007).

21 James Epstein, '"Our real constitution": Trial defence and radical memory in the Age of Revolution' in James Vernon (ed.), *Re-reading the Constitution* (Cambridge, 1996), pp.31–46.

22 Edmund S. Morgan, *Inventing the People: The Rise of Popular Sovereignty in England and America* (New York, 1988), pp.12–15 and *passim*.

23 For rather different views of Mansfield's actions and intentions, see George van Cleve, 'Somerset's case and its antecedents in imperial perspective', *Law and History Review* 24 (2006); and Anthony Lester and Geoffrey Bindman, *Race and Law* (London, 1972), pp.28–34. A verdict that 'the state of slavery' was 'not recognized by the laws of this kingdom' was also given in the case of Joseph Knight (a formerly enslaved African) *v.* John Wedderburn in the Court of Session in Edinburgh in 1777–8.

24 See my *Britons*, pp.350–60; and Christopher Brown, *Moral Capital: Foundations of British Abolitionism* (Chapel Hill, NC, 2006).

25 See David Armitage, *The Ideological Origins of the British Empire* (Cambridge, 2000); and B. Ibhawoh, 'Stronger than the maxim gun: human rights and British colonial hegemony in Nigeria', *Africa: Journal of the International African Institute* 72 (2002).

26 For how the business of empire could result in British and Irish participants themselves being captured, and the consequences of this for arguments and myths about liberty and freedom, see my *Captives: Britain, Empire and the World 1600–1850* (London, 2002).

27 Though the rule of law has been flouted within Britain itself rather more than is commonly realized or officially proclaimed: see, for instance, K.D. Ewing and C.A. Gearty (eds.), *The Struggle for Civil Liberties: Political Freedom and the Rule of Law in Britain 1914–1945* (Oxford, 2000).

28 Quoted in Linebaugh, *Magna Carta*, pp.145–6.

29 Brian Simpson, *Human Rights and the End of Empire, passim*.

30 Isaiah Berlin, 'Two concepts of liberty' in his *Four Essays on Liberty* (Oxford, 1969); but see Quentin Skinner, 'A third concept of liberty', *Proceedings of the British Academy* 117 (2002).

31 Vernon Bogdanor, *Devolution in the United Kingdom* (Oxford, 2001).

32 James E. Cronin, *The Politics of State Expansion: War, State and Society in Twentieth-Century Britain* (London, 1991), p.120.

33 Edward Higgs, *The Information State in England: The Central Collection of Information on Citizens Since 1500* (Basingstoke, 2004), p.4 and *passim*. As Higgs points out, information gathering is not always or necessarily the same as surveillance.

34 See Gordon Wood, 'The History of Rights in Early America', in B.A. Shain (ed.), *The Nature of Rights at the American Founding and Beyond* (London, 2007), pp.233–57.

35 Lord Scarman, *Why Britain Needs a Written Constitution* (London, 1992), p.7; John Douglas, quoted in John Guy, 'The "imperial crown" and the liberty of the subject' in B.Y. Kunze and D.D. Brautigan (eds.), *Court, Country and Culture: Essays on Early Modern British History in Honor of Perez Zagorin* (Rochester, NY, 1992), p.87.

36 For useful introductions to the lives and work of these men, and suggestions for further reading on their copious and complex writings and speeches, see the biographies in the online version of the *Oxford Dictionary of National Biography* (http://www.oxforddnb.com); for their protracted influence on the British 'official mind', see Chapter 1 of Anthony Lester and David Pannick (eds.), *Human Rights Law and Practice* (2nd edn., London, 2004).

37 See the online version of a speech in June 2007 by Trevor Phillips 'Britain's new commission for equality and human rights: challenge and opportunities' in which he discusses media reactions to the HRA (http://www.equalityhumanrights.com); Lester and Bindman, *Race and Law*, p.414.

38 Lord Scarman, *Why Britain Needs a Written Constitution*, p.4.

List of Exhibits

LIBERTY AND THE RULE OF LAW

1 Magna Carta, 1215 (British Library, Cotton MS Augustus ii.106).

2 *Charta de Foresta*, Law of the Forests, Westminster, 11 Febr. 9 Hen. III., 1225 (British Library, Add.Ch.24712).

3 Laws of Hywel Dda, *c.*1230–82 (National Library of Wales, Peniarth MS 28, ff.1v–2).

4 The 'Ayr Manuscript', Acts of the Scottish Parliament, 1318 (National Archives of Scotland, PA5/2).

5 Edward Coke, *The Second Part of the Institutes of the Lawes of England*, London, 1642 (British Library, 508.f.9).

6 William Blackstone, *The Great Charter and Charter of the Forest...*, Oxford, 1759 (British Library, 676.h.3).

7 *The Great Charter called i[n] latyn Magna Carta...*, London [1541?] (British Library, C.40.c.71(1)).

8 *An Act for the Better Securing the Liberty of the Subject, and for Prevention of Imprisonments Beyond the Seas...*' (Habeas Corpus Act), London [1679] (British Library, BS.Ref 3/15).

9 Print of Sun Yatsen, souvenir of the Guomindang's (Nationalist) Northern Expedition (1926) Guomin gemingjun beifaji, photolithographic poster in the style of 'New Year' woodblock prints, Shanghai, *c.*1927 (British Library, Or.5896).

10 Sun Yatsen's application for admission to the British Museum Reading Room, 1889 [1896] (British Museum Archives).

11 Sun Yatsen's application for admission to the British Museum Reading Room, 1905 (British Museum Archives).

12 Wên Sun [Sun Yatsen], *Kidnapped in London: Being the Story of My Capture by, Detention at, and Release from the Chinese Legation, London*, Bristol, 1897 (British Library, 10606.aaa.33).

13 T.J. Wooler, *Black Dwarf*, London, 1817, poster of the death of Habeas Corpus, 'Alas poor H.C.' (British Library, PP.3612.acb).

14 T.J. Wooler, *Black Dwarf*, London, 1817 (British Library, PP.3612.acb).

15 T.J. Wooler, *Black Dwarf*, London, 1817, poster, 'Trial by Jury!' (British Library, PP.3612.acb).

PARLIAMENT AND THE PEOPLE

16 Petition of Right, 1628 (Parliamentary Archives, HL/PO/PU/1/1627/3C1n2).

17 Cambridgeshire petition against episcopacy, 1641 (British Library, Egerton MS 1048 ff.24 and 25).

18 Images of civil war banners (British Library, Add. MS 5247, f.47).

19 The death warrant of Charles I, 1649 (Parliamentary Archives, HL/PO/JO/10/297A).

20 John Leicester, *England's Miraculous Preservation Emblematically Described...*, London, 1646, print

(British Library, 669.f.10 (107)).

21 *The Headless Horseman,* print by Pierre Lombart after Anthony Van Dyck, 1633; the horseman is Charles I (British Museum Prints & Drawings, P,2.48).

22 *The Headless Horseman*, print by Pierre Lombart after Anthony Van Dyck, after 1655; the horseman is Oliver Cromwell (British Museum Prints & Drawings, P,4.32).

23 *The Headless Horseman*, print by Pierre Lombart after Anthony Van Dyck, after 1655; the horseman has his face erased (British Museum Prints & Drawings, P,2.49).

24 *Act Declaring the People of England to be a Commonwealth and Free State...*', 1649 (The National Archives, C204/9).

25 'The Great Seal of England in the First Year of Freedom by God's Blessing Restored', 1648, two examples of the seal showing obverse and reverse (British Library, Add.Ch.34941 and Add. MS 3243B).

26 Henry Marten, 'Fundamentall rights belonging to the English nation', n.d. (British Library, Add. MS 71534, f.15).

27 The Putney Debates, 1647 (Worcester College, Oxford University, Oxford MS 65 ff.34v–35).

28 'An agreement of the People of England', 1649 (British Library, Egerton MS 1048, f.91).

29 Thomas Hobbes, 'Leviathan, or the matter, forme and power of a common-wealth ecclesiasticall and civil... ', 1651 (British Library, Egerton MS 1910).

30 Oath taken by Oliver Cromwell as Lord Protector, 26 June, 1657 (British Library, Egerton MS 1048, f.115).

31 *The Government of the Common-wealth of England, Scotland & Ireland...*, London, 1653 (British Library, G.4962).

32 Thomas Simon's designs for the Cromwellian coinage, 1656 (British Museum Prints & Drawings, 1987, 0725.28).

33 Thomas Simon's drawings for the Great Seal of Charles II, Whitehall, 2 October 1662 (British Library Add. MS 71450).

34 Romeyn de Hooge, 'Wilhelmus Rex, & Maria Regina. 1688', etching, 1688 (British Library, 504.l.10 (19)).

35 Bill of Rights, 1689 (Parliamentary Archives).

THE RIGHT TO VOTE

36 William Hogarth, *Four Prints of an Election*: 1. *An Election Entertainment*, London, 1755; 2. *Canvassing for Votes*, London, 1757; 3. *The Polling*, London, 1758; 4. *Chairing the Members*, London, 1758 (British Museum, Prints & Drawings, S,2.130, 131, 133 and 135).

37 A bill for election cockades, 1790; and a bill for election expenses, 1796 (British Library Bowood Papers, B71, ff.5 and 13).

38 John Fletcher, 'This bill opposes no candidate...', Southampton, 1831 (British Library, H.S.74/1549 (175)).

39 J. Coupland, 'All hands a-hoy!...', Southampton, 1831

(British Library, H.S.74/1549 (183)).

40 Minute book of the London Corresponding Society, London, 2 April 1792 (British Library, Add. MS 27812, f.2v).

41 Handbill advocating support for Burdett and Kinnaird in the 1818 election (British Library, Add. MS 27846, ff.8–9).

42 *The Political 'A, Apple-Pie;'...*, London, 1820 (British Library C.131.d.10 (6)).

43 *Report of the Metropolitan and Central Committee Appointed for the Relief of the Manchester Sufferers...*, London, 1820 (British Library, RB.23.b.4235 (1)).

44 *The Political House that Jack Built...*, 16th edition, London, 1819 (British Library, 8135.e.1 (6)).

45 John Bull, *The Palace of John Bull Contrasted with the Poor House that Jack Built,* London, 1820 (British Library, C.131.d.13 (2)).

46 Reform Act, 1832 (Parliamentary Archives, HL/PO/PU/1/ 1832/2&3W4n147).

47 Poster signed by Wellington and others opposing the Reform Bill, 1832 (British Library, Add. MS 27792, f.300).

48 'The Black list:...who voted against the Reform Bill...', 8 October, 1831 (British Library, 826.l.28 (6)).

49 John Frederick Herring Junior, bound sketchbook entitled 'Flights of Fancy...Jany. 1. 1831' (British Library, Add. MS 74284, f.138).

50 Thomas Walter Williams, *Parliamentary Reform...*, London, 1832 (British Library, 1490.de.41).

51 E. Wallis, *A New Plan of Brighton and Kemp-Town*, c.1832–35+ (British Library, Maps C.44.d.19).

52 'The Bells are a' ringing' [Edinburgh, 1832] (British Library, 826.l.28(66)).

53 J.M.W. Turner, *The Northampton Election, 6 December 1830*, c.1830–1, watercolour, gouache and pen and ink on paper (Tate Britain, T12321).

54 Reform Act Medal, 1832 (People's History Museum, NMLH.1995.91.59).

55 'Handbill of the National political union', 1831 (British Library Add. MS 27791, f.46).

56 The minutes of the Working Men's Association, 1836–39 (British Library, Add. MS 37773, ff.16v–17).

57 *The People's Charter: Being the Outline of An Act to Provide for the Just Representation of the People of Great Britain...in Parliament...*, London [1838] (British Library, C.194.a.938).

58 Letter of the Working Men's Association of Ashburton, 27 February 1839 (British Library, Add. MS 34245A, f.74).

59 *Interesting Life, and Important Eight Day's Trial of John Frost...*, Leeds, 1840 (British Library, 1578/805(1)).

60 Thomas Cooper, 'The Purgatory of Suicides', 1842–44 (British Library, Add. MS 56238, ff.3 and 4).

61 Ernest Jones, 'Album of sketches, verses...', 1843–53: 'The Grecian City & The English Town' (British Library, Add. MS 61971, ff.28v–29).

62 Commemorative jug depicting Ernest Jones, date unknown (People's History Museum, NMLH.1995.91.9).

63 Chartist 'truncheon' table leg, date unknown (People's History Museum, NMLH.2005.33.4).

64 Printed funeral card, 1877, and photograph of William Lovett, probably 1870s (British Library Add. MS 78164A, ff.4 and 42).

65 *National Union of Women's Suffrage Societies*, London, 1909 (British Library, 8413.k.5).

66 Letter from Annie Kenney to Arthur Balfour, 30 January 1910 (British Library Add. MS 49793, f.127).

67 Letter from Christabel Pankhurst to Henry Devenish Harben, August 1913 (British Library, Add. MS 58226, f.26).

68 'Panko' card game, c.1911 (Women's Library, 7JCC).

69 Emily Davison's purse and tickets, 1913 (Women's Library, 7RMB/A24).

70 Arncliffe-Sennet scrapbooks; items relating to the death of Emily Davison, 1913 (British Library, C.121.g.1, vol.23).

71 Poster advertising *The Suffragette*, London, 1913–14 (British Library, LB.31.b.7394).

72 Notebook of Olive Wharry, 1911–14 and 1928 (British Library, Add. MS 49976, ff.64v–65).

73 Rosa May Billinghurst's account of her time in prison (Women's Library, 7RMB/A24 a & b).

74 Ida Mary Buchanan, diary, 18 March 1913 (British Library, Add. MS 62699, ff.79–80).

75 Leaflet advertising Kingsway Hall meeting to protest against force feeding, 18 March 1918 (British Library, Add. MS 50701, f.222).

76 Elsie Duval's hunger strike medal, date unknown (Women's Library, 7HFD/D/17).

77 'Votes for Women' doll with pins stuck into it, date unknown (National History Museum Wales, F07.6).

78 Walter Burton Baldry, *From Hampstead to Holloway...*, London, 1909 (British Library, 12331.k.26).

UNITED KINGDOM?

79 Matthew Paris, *Map of Great Britain, c.AD 1250* (British Library, Cotton MS Claudius D.VI, f.12).

80 The Bull of Pope Honorius III affirming the independence of the Church in Scotland from any jurisdiction except that of the Roman pontiff or his legate *a latere*, 21 November 1218 (National Archives of Scotland, RH5/3).

81 'Award of Norham', 1291 (British Library, Cotton Ch.XVIII.40).

82 The Declaration of Arbroath, 1320 (British Library, Royal MS 13 E. X, ff. 207v–208).

83 Acts of the Scottish Parliament, 1425 (National Archives of Scotland PA5/6).

84 Edward I and his court, c.1280–1300 (British Library, Cotton MS Vitellius A.XIII, f.6v).

85 Pennal Letter, 1406; le charte scellee of Owain Glyndŵr and letter of Owain Glyndŵr to Charles VI of France, 1406 (Archives National de France, Paris, J//516/A/29 and J//516/B/40).

86 The Irish Remonstrance of 1317 (British Library, Harl. MS 712, ff.210v–211).

87 Chronicle of Mann, describing a meeting of the Tynewald in 1237 (British Library, Cotton MS Julius A.VII, ff.44v–45).

88 *Angliae Figura*, 1540 (British Library, Cotton MS Augustus 1.i.9).

89 Treaty of Union, 1604 (The National Archives, PRO 30/49).

90 Proposed designs for the Union flag, 1604 (National Library of Scotland, MS 2517, f.67v).

91 Scottish National Covenant, 1638 (National Library of Scotland, Adv MS 20.6.15).

92 Images of Scots banners captured at Preston, 1648, and at Dunbar, 1650 (British Library, Harl. MS 1460, ff.33v–34).

93 Articles of Union, 1706 (National Archives of Scotland, SP13/209).

94 Designs by Sir Henry St George of the reformed Royal Standard and Union flag after the Union of 1707 (Private Collection).

95 Jacobite cockade found on the battlefield after Culloden, 1746 (British Library, Add. MS 35889, f.108).

96 Tom Merry, *Home Rule Procession at Scarborough Broken up 4th July 1892*, 1893, print (British Museum, Prints & Drawings, 1893,0320.2).

97 Notes used by Gladstone to introduce the Home Rule Bill, 1893 (British Library, Add. MS 39927, f.68).

98 Home Rule Council, *The ABC Home Rule Handbook*, London, 1912 (British Library, 8146.f.3).

99 Flyer for National Protest meeting against Home Rule, 14 June 1912 (British Library, Add. MS 62435, f.51).

100 Text of the King's speech at the opening of the Buckingham House conference, 21 July 1914 (British Library, Lansdowne Papers, uncatalogued).

101 *Sinn Fein Rebellion Handbook, Easter 1916*, compiled by the *Weekly Irish Times*, Dublin, 1917 (British Library, YA. 1990.b.1181).

102 David Low, 'An Unforgettable Sight', a study for a cartoon first published in the *Evening Standard*, 17 May 1932 (British Museum, Prints & Drawings, 1934,0811.5).

103 John Saunders Lewis, *Egwyddorion Cenedlaetholdeb*, Machynlleth, 1935 (British Library, 08139.d.16).

104 Douglas Young, *'Fascism for the Highlands'? Gauleiter for Wales?...* , Glasgow, 1943 (British Library, X.709/746).

105 Oliver Brown, *Scotlandshire, England's Worst-governed Province*, Milngavie, 1948 (British Library, 8142.b.71).

106 *The Belfast Agreement,* 1997–98 (British Library, Cm 3883*).*

HUMAN RIGHTS

107 John Locke, *Two Treatises of Government:...*, London, 1690 (British Library, C.107.e.89).

108 John Locke's draft of the Carolina constitution (The National Archives, PRO 30/24/47/3).

109 Fragment of the unsigned will of Jean-Jacques Rousseau, 27 May 1766 (British Library, Add. MS 29627, f. 1).

110 *Déclaration des droits de l'homme et du citoyen...*, Paris, 1791 (British Library, R.148(9)).

111 *In Congress, July 4, 1776. A Declaration by the Representatives of the United States of America, in General Congress Assembled,* New York printing of the Declaration of Independence (The National Archives, CO 5/177, f.29, excerpt 976).

112 Thomas Paine, *Rights of Man:...*, London, 1791 (British Library, 523.f.19).

113 Thomas Paine, *Rights of Man: Part the Second...*, London, 1792 (British Library C.115.e.2(3)).

114 William Blake, notebook containing autograph drafts of poems and prose, c.1787–1818 (British Library, Add. MS 49460, f.56).

115 J. Mason, letter on Thomas Paine's flight (British Library, Add. MS 58968, f.67).

116 Edmund Burke, *Reflection on the Revolution in France,* London, 1790 (British Library, 1059.i.24).

117 *The Contrast: 1792. English Liberty, French Liberty... Which is Best?,* 1792 (British Library, 648.c.26(28)).

118 James Gillray, *Patriotic Regeneration, –viz.– Parliament Reform'd, a la Francoise...*, London, 1795, satirical print (British Museum, Prints & Drawings, 1868, 0808.10376).

119 'Subversive tobacco paper', 1792 (British Library, Add. MS 16,922, f.1).

120 Mary Wollstonecraft, *A Vindication of the Rights of Woman:...*, London, 1792 (British Library, 523.g.3).

121 John Opie, *Portrait of Mary Wollstonecraft, c.*1790–1, oil on canvas (Tate Britain, N01167).

122 'John Stuart Mill on the Black Act', 1838 (British Library, Add. MS 36468, f.406).

123 'Fair Minutes of the Committee for the Abolition of the Slave Trade' (British Library, Add. MS 21254, f.2).

124 'Am I not a Man and a Brother', token, after 1797 (People's History Museum, NMLH.1995.91.46, aft.1787).

125 Robert Wedderburn, *The Horrors of Slavery:...*, London, 1824 (British Library, 8156.c.71(4)).

126 Letter from Montenegrin Red Cross, 26 July 1916 (British Library Add. MS 46014, f.25).

127 Letter from Rene Cassin to Lord Cecil, 24 April 1934; and letter from Cecil to Cassin, 25 April 1934 (British Library, Add. MS 51169, ff.107 and 112).

128 *Atlantic Charter* [Utrecht], 1944 (British Library, Cup.406.a.9).

129 *A Declaration of the Rights of Man. A Charter Prepared by a Committee under the Chairmanship of Lord Sankey...*, London, 1947 (British Library, 08286.m.33).

130 Clifford Hulme, *San Francisco Conference*, London, 1945 (British Library, 8011.a.62).

131 Dorothea Fisher, *A Fair World for All. The Meaning of the Declaration of Human Rights...*, with a foreword by Eleanor Roosevelt, illustrated by Jeanne Bendick, New York, 1952 (British Library, 8011.c.45).

132 United Nations, *Universal Declaration of Human Rights...Final Authorized Text*, Lake Success, 1949 (British Library, UNA.500/19).

133 Secret circular dispatch on the Universal Declaration of Human Rights from Arthur Creech Jones, 28 March 1949 (The National Archives, CO 537/4580).

134 Letter dated 12 May 1949 to Arthur Creech Jones from Government House, Sierra Leone, raising concerns over the Universal Declaration of Human Rights (The National Archives, CO 537/4580).

135 Letter dated 29 April 1949 to Arthur Creech Jones from the West Indies raising concerns over the Universal Declaration of Human Rights (The National Archives, CO 537/4580).

136 Human Rights Act, 1998 (British Library, BS.Ref.3 1998 pt.III).

137 Race Relations Act, 1965 (British Library, BS.Ref.3. 1965 pt.II).

138 *Home Office Report of the Committee on Homosexual Offences and Prostitution*, London, 1957 (British Library B.S.Ref 1/14).

139 'Outrage!, "Homophobia Kills"', placard, after 1999 (British Library, uncatalogued).

140 'Outrage!, "Queer Remembrance"', flier, 1993 (British Library, uncatalogued).

141 John Stuart Mill, *On Liberty*, London, 1859 (British Library C.60.k.12).

FREEDOM FROM WANT

142 'Articles of Agreement between the members of the Seamen's Loyal Standard Association for Tyne & Wear...', South Shields, 1825 (British Library, Add. MS 27803, f.127).

143 'Whereas it has been humbly represented...a considerable number of persons did...unlawfully and riotously assemble...the river Wear and its banks...', Sunderland [1825], [proclamation by Robert Peel offering £100 reward] (British Library, Add. MS 27803, f.91).

144 'Statement of the accounts of the South Shields Seamen's Loyal Standard Association', 1826 (British Library, Add. MS 27803, f.138).

145 'Chartist survey of national social and economic conditions', Bradford, May 1839 (British Library, Add. MS 34245B, f.280).

146 'To the non-signers of Bradford and its neighbourhood', Bradford [1825] (British Library, Add. MS 27803, f.328).

147 *An Original Portrait of Captain Swing*, London, c.1830, hand-coloured lithograph (British Museum, Prints & Drawings, 1997,0928.30).

148 *O'Connorville the first estate purchased by the Chartist Co-operative Land Company...founded by Feargus O'Connor Esqr 1846*, hand-coloured map (British Library, Maps.162.s.1).

149 Letter of Hubert Bland to George Bernard Shaw inviting him to join the Fabian Society (British Library, Add. MS 50557, ff.1v–2).

150 The Fabian Society, 'Why are the Many Poor?', London, 1884 [Fabian Tracts no.1] (British Library, Add. MS 50557, ff.1v–2).

151 Draft terms of agreement in hand of John Burns following the great dock strike of 1889 (British Library, Add. MS 46286, ff.47v–48).

152 H. Llewellyn Smith, Vaughan Nash, *The Story of the Dockers' Strike*, London, [1889]; [John Burns' copy] (British Library, Add. MS 74265B).

153 Charles Booth, *Descriptive Map of London Poverty 1889*, London, 1891 (British Library, Maps C.21.a.18.(295) (south east sheet)).

154 Letter from John Burns to Herbert Asquith, 11 May 1910 (British Library, Add. MS 46282, f.102).

155 National Insurance stamps, 1912 (British Library, Philatelic Collections, Board of Inland Revenue, Stamping Department Archive).

156 Anti-Socialist Union to John Burns, 29 Nov 1910 (British Library, Add. MS 74260, f.64).

157 Correspondence concerning the parliamentary crisis, 1911 (British Library, Lansdowne Papers, uncatalogued).

158 Budget League poster depicting Britannia and a Peer (People's History Museum, NMLH. 1994.168.308).

159 *Daily Mirror*, 12 May 1926, General Strike edition (British Library, Western Manuscripts, uncatalogued).

160 John Maynard Keynes and H.D. Henderson, *Can Lloyd George Do It?...*, London [1929] (British Library, 011824.d.45).

161 The Next Five Years Group, *A Summary of the Book 'The Next Five Years': An Essay in Political Agreement*, London, 1936 (British Library, 08139.d.47).

162 Letter from Paul Emrys-Evans to Clement Atlee, 24 April 1957 (British Library, Add. MS 58247, f.43).

163 Herbert Morrison, *Mr Smith and Mr Schmidt*, London, [1940] (British Library, 1899.ss.18 (14)).

164 Walter Padley, *The Real Battle for Britain*, London, 1943, Independent Labour Party pamphlet (British Library, 1899.ss.3 (31)).

165 The Labour Party, *Your Future. After Victory – What Then?* (British Library, 1899.ss.6 (52)).

166 Ellen Wilkinson, *Plan for Peace,* London, 1945 (British Library, 08138.aa.34).

167 Waldron Smithers, *Socialism Offers Slavery,* 1945 (British Library, 1899.ss.11 (9)).

168 'Help them finish the job', Labour Party poster, 1945 (People's History Museum, NMLH.1995.39).

169 'Report by Sir William Beveridge, Social Insurance and Allied Services', London, 1942 (British Library, BS.Ref 1/1942–43 vi.119, Cmnd 6404).

170 Letter from Sir William Beveridge to Roy Harrod, 15 September, 1944 (British Library, Add. MS 71182, f.4).

171 Ronald Conway Davison, *Protezione sociale in Gran Bretagna…,* London, 1944 (British Library, 8287.i.41).

172 William Beveridge, *Social Insurance and Allied Services,* [The Netherlands, 1944], clandestinely published (British Library, Cup.21.p.22).

173 William Beveridge, *Der Beveridgeplan,* Zurich, 1943 (British Library, F10/5052).

174 Letter from R.A. Butler to Marie Stopes concerning the Education Act, 21 October 1943 (British Library, Add. MS 58726, f.142).

175 Barbara Drake, *Education,* London [1944] (British Library 899.ss.6 (50)).

176 G.D.H. Cole, *How to Obtain Full Employment,* London, [1944] (British Library, 1899.ss.6 (45)).

177 J.L. Smyth, *Social Security,* London [1944] (British Library, 1899.ss.6 (51)).

178 *Your Health Service. How It Will Work in Scotland,* Edinburgh, 1948 (British Library, 7391.t.53).

179 Millicent Bouverie, *Daily Mail Book of Post-War Homes,* London [1944] (British Library, 7822.bbb.12).

FREEDOM OF SPEECH AND BELIEF

180 *The Holy Bible…,* London, 1611, the first edition of the King James' Bible, or 'Authorized' version (British Library, C.35.l.13).

181 'Test Act certificate', 1673 (British Library, Add. MS 36526B, f.11).

182 *An Act for Exempting their Majesties Protestant Subjects, Dissenting from the Church of England, from the Penalties of Certain Laws…,* London, 1689; [The Act of Toleration], 1689 (British Library, BS.Ref. 3 (1688–89)).

183 Quaker marriage certificate of William Storrs Fry, 1767 (British Library, Egerton Ch.8842).

184 Printed handbill issued at the time of Gordon Riots, 1780 (British Library, 1855.c.4(67)).

185 Sketch by T. Foley showing military encampments, 1780 (British Library, Add. MS 23940, f.62).

186 Susan Burney, 'An eyewitness account of Gordon Riots', 1780 (British Library, Egerton MS 3691, f.132).

187 Map of Munster, 1828 (British Library, Add. MS 63632).

188 Petition by Manasseh ben Israel and others to Cromwell asking for Jews to have the right to practice their religion, 1656 (The National Archives, SP 18/125, f.173).

189 Rembrandt, *Samuel Manasseh Ben Israel,* 1636, etched print (British Museum, Prints & Drawings, 1982,U.2711).

190 John Ruslen, silver dish, 1702, emblem of London, Spanish and Portuguese synagogues (Jewish Museum, JM 656).

191 List of Jews in London, c.1658–60 (British Library, Add. MS 29868, f.15).

192 John Aynsley, ceramic jug commemorating the boxer Daniel Mendoza, 1800 (Jewish Museum, JM 686).

193 Petition to Sir Robert Peel from English Jews protesting against the stigma of discrimination, 1845 (British Library, Add. MS 40612, ff.163v–164).

194 *Salomons & Gladstone for Greenwich…,* London, c.1868, election poster (British Library, Add. MS 44798, ff.104–105).

195 John Milton, *Areopagitica,* London, 1644 (British Library, Ashley 1176).

196 William Hogarth, *John Wilkes Esqr.,* 1763, etched and engraved print (British Museum, Prints & Drawings, Cc,2.206).

197 Letter from John Wilkes to John Almon (British Library, Add. MS 30868, f.157).

198 *The Debates and Proceedings of the British House of Commons, during the…Sessions…1743–1774,* compiled by J. Almon et al. (British Library, 289.d.1).

199 Richard Baines, Note concerning…Christopher Marlowe, 1593 (British Library, Harley MS 6848, f.185v).

200 Material relating to the Oz obscenity trial at the Old Bailey, London 1971 (British Library, RG.2000.b.17).

201 Ernest Pack, *The Trial and Imprisonment of J. Gott for Blasphemy,* Bradford, 1911 (British Library, X.208/112).

202 *Conference on the Official Secrets Acts and the Freedom of the Press,* London [1938] (British Library, YD.2006.a.4049).

203 Compton Mackenzie, *Greek Memories,* London, 1932 (British Library, Cup.410.f. 383).

204 *The 'D' Notice System. Presented to the Parliament by the Prime Minister,* 1967 (British Library, BS.68/152).

205 Spies for Peace, *Danger! Official Secret, RSG-6,* London, 1963 (British Library, LB.31.c.7703 (1–3)).

206 Peter Wright, *Spionjeger,* Bergen, 1987 (British Library, Cup.719/816).

207 Peter Hedley, *The 'D' Notice Affair,* London, 1967 (British Library, X.709/6022).